The Plutarch Primer

Publicola

(Revised)

by

Anne E. White

Table of Contents

Getting Started With Plutarch (and Publicola in particular)

Is Plutarch Hard?

Have you heard that old story about people who moved to a new neighborhood that they'd been told was the friendliest place in the world? It turned out that their informants were right. They smiled at everyone, everyone smiled back, and they made friends right away. But another couple heard that the same neighborhood was a bad, unfriendly place to live, and, strangely enough, that's what they found too.

Like that neighborhood, Plutarch has gotten a bad rap among homeschoolers. For some, his *Lives* have taken on the mountain-climbing quality of Senior Chemistry. Studying the leaders of another culture and time is not an easy task even for adults; how do we expect students aged ten to fourteen to make sense of this?

Well...many of us learned Bible stories as children, didn't we? Sunday school teachers have no hesitation about plowing through the Kings of the Old Testament, or telling about Paul's adventures around the Mediterranean. Many of us remember small classrooms with large, slightly worn wall maps of the Red Sea and pictures of Solomon's Temple. We may not have been clear on the Babylonians' fall to the Persians, or known exactly where Ephesus was, but we knew about Daniel and the lions, and about Jonah not wanting to go to Nineveh.

1

Many of the people Plutarch wrote about are not totally unfamiliar either. Everybody knows Julius Caesar (and Brutus, and Marc Antony, each of whom has his own *Life*). Everybody's heard of Alexander the Great. Those who have read mythology know Romulus and Theseus. We may not know Fabius, but we've heard (even vaguely) about his enemy Hannibal (didn't he come over the Alps? Something about elephants?). We recognize references to Athens and Sparta. Most adults probably know more about Greek and Roman history and culture than we give ourselves credit for. And what we don't know, we can always look up.

Then is it the writing, the language, the style that frightens people off before they get started? Yes, somewhat. Plutarch wrote almost two thousand years ago, in a serious, aimed-at-adults style. His early translators into English used the language in ways that sometimes seem to need a translation in themselves. (There *are* modern English translations of Plutarch, for those who just want the stories without sixteenth- or seventeenth-century decorations.)

I hear someone objecting, "I can handle this, but I'm an adult! Remember, I have to be able to teach it to an eleven-year-old!" As Charlotte Mason said, we read a little at a time, and go slow.

When we teach Bible stories, we focus on the narrative and the people involved. How did they trust in God? What mistakes did they make? How did their choices affect other people down the road? Many reading John Bunyan's *The Pilgrim's Progress* have adopted the creative narration strategy (described briefly in *For the Children's Sake*) of having their students draw a scene from each lesson on a paper scroll. (Christian, in the story, carried a scroll with him). When we look at a passage from Plutarch, we can imagine something similar: what would we draw on a scroll or page for this story? What could we add to a mental map? (Real maps are useful too.) Without belaboring the moral of a story (as Mason cautions us not to do), what points of character might be brought out?

I want to add one more thought here to the question of "difficulty." On the AmblesideOnline Forum, people were discussing getting started with a particular *Life*. One member piped up, "I didn't know that was supposed to be one of the more difficult ones! We're just reading it, and having no problems!" Like Senior Chemistry, if nobody tells you that it's supposed to be impossible, maybe it won't be.

Why Plutarch?

The decision to include Plutarch's *Lives*—or not—or in what translation—becomes a kind of touchpoint for how we view (or do) a Charlotte Mason education. Shakespeare is easy; everyone knows Shakespeare, recognizes Shakespeare. Nobody argues with teaching Shakespeare. But Plutarch belongs much more unmistakably to Charlotte Mason. If homeschooling was the world and Charlotte Mason was Canada, Plutarch would be maple syrup. We need to ask, and it's a fair question, if this was just one of those quaint turn-of-the-century ideas, like making Smyrna rugs for handicrafts; if Plutarch's *Lives* is essential in itself, or if what it offers could more easily be acquired through newer books. Why did Charlotte Mason include this particular piece of antiquity?

Here are some of the reasons that Mason gave herself, or that were noted by her colleagues:

1) In the preface to *Ourselves*, she wrote that the novels of Sir Walter Scott and Plutarch's *Lives* were "sources that fall within everybody's reading." This is obviously not the case now, but at one time, Plutarch was considered common currency. Shakespeare read Plutarch. Abraham Lincoln read Plutarch. Frankenstein's monster read Plutarch. Ralph Waldo Emerson begins his essay on Plutarch with the words, "It is remarkable that of an author so familiar as Plutarch, not only to scholars, but to all reading men..." Plutarch is not studied in most contemporary schools, at least below university level, but he was less obscure in previous eras than we may realize.

2) Similarly, the introduction of Plutarch at what seems a younger-than-necessary age was explained in *Parents and Children*[1] as part of a plan that brings a child to the world's library door, and offers him the key to its contents. (It is worth noting that Mason mentions only two books in that passage: *Tanglewood Tales* for young children, and then Plutarch's *Lives*.) We don't just hand the child these books; we read them to him, but without too much explanation, a gift from one book-loving friend to another. We read, he narrates, we discuss, but we do not limit what he learns

to our own ideas about it. These prepared notes might seem to be at cross-purposes with Mason's "pick it up and read" attitude, but I justify them with the hope that they will encourage those of us who did not grow up with Plutarch.

3) As well as an early beginning to literature and the habit of reading in general, Plutarch offers "the best preparation for the study of Grecian or of Roman history."[2] Note that Mason said preparation for history, not history itself. It is a familiarizing, a paving of the way. After reading several *Lives*, we begin to recognize not only the characters, but also places, events, and cultural details such as the election of Roman consuls.

4) The book *In Memoriam* says that Charlotte Mason lived during an age that was fascinated by history, but that her "standards of judgement were ethical" and that "greatness in goodness was her ideal..."[3] Miss Ambler, the author of a *Parents' Review* article on teaching Plutarch, agreed:

> We need, however, to have more than a goal in view; we need to know the way to reach it. We know what is necessary for a good citizen, and we wish to send the children out equipped for service with high ideals and the courage to live up to them.[4]

Using the Lesson Material

These notes, and the accompanying text, are prepared for the use of individual students and small groups following a twelve-week school term. Each study contains explanatory material before the first lesson. A little at the beginning may be useful to stir interest in the study, but it is not meant to be given all in one dose!

I encourage you to make the lessons your own. Use the questions that are the most meaningful to you. Remember that Charlotte Mason was satisfied with "Proper names are written on the blackboard, and then the children narrate what they have listened to."

She also emphasized the importance of recapitulation, which can have two meanings: beginning each lesson by remembering what has gone before; or recalling something already known, and emphasizing particular points at the end of a lesson, which (again) should help with the next one. Some of the Creative Narration suggestions may help to "cement" these stories in the students' memories, as well as to bring out interesting new points and possibilities.

Translations and Vocabulary

The text is a free mixture of Thomas North's 1579 translation of *Plutarch's Lives of the Noble Greeks and Romans* and John Dryden's 1683 translation. (Dryden for clarity, North for character.) Omissions have been made for length and suitability, for the intended age group.

An expression that comes up in *Publicola* (**Lesson Eleven**) is "making virtue of necessity." Instead of worrying about the hard words in Plutarch, let's celebrate the richness of our language! The lists of vocabulary words are mainly for reference rather than drill or homework. Charlotte Mason mentions teaching a few necessary words before beginning a story; which ones you choose will depend on the students' needs. Often that would include words for unfamiliar types of buildings or weapons, which could be shown with pictures. My choice of these as a teacher would often be words that might have changed meaning or be otherwise ambiguous. One of my children's memorable Plutarch moments involved escaping slaves who (providentially) discovered a cartload of "arms" with which they "flew."

Examination Questions

Sample examination questions follow the final lesson; these can be incorporated into term examinations. Since we do not currently have access to original notes for a term of Publicola, these have been created for this study.

How would Charlotte Mason have taught a Plutarch lesson?

The simplest description of a "regular" lesson in Plutarch is given in

Charlotte Mason's 1907 book *School Education*:

> Plutarch's *Lives* are read in Classes II. and III., and as children are usually five years in these two classes, they may read some fifteen of these *Lives*...The *Lives* are read to the children almost without comment, but with necessary omissions. Proper names are written on the blackboard, and then the children narrate what they have listened to.

In her later book *Philosophy of Education,* she added,

> So far as we can get them we use expurgated editions [edited for school use]; in other cases the book is read aloud by the teacher with necessary omissions.

There are two sample Plutarch lessons in the Appendices of *School Education*. One of those is an introduction to Alexander the Great, which brings out several useful points about character, but is not an everyday lesson; it is meant "to introduce the boys to a fresh hero." Teaching points include "connecting Alexander the Great with the time of Demosthenes, of whom the boys have been learning recently"; starting with an interesting story of Alexander's boyhood, and drawing out character qualities illustrated by that story; and showing a map "illustrating his campaigns."

The other lesson is labelled "Narration," rather than "History," but it may reflect more of the lesson style described above.

> OBJECTS.
>
> 1. To improve the children's power of narration by impressing on them Plutarch's style (as translated by North), and making them narrate as much as possible in his words.
>
> 2. To rouse in the children admiration of Alexander's love of simplicity, generosity, and kindness to his men.
>
> LESSON.
>
> Step 1. Connect with the last lesson by questioning

the children. They read last time stories illustrating Alexander's graciousness and tact.

Step 2. Tell the children shortly the substance of what I am going to read to them, letting them find any places mentioned, in their maps.

Step 3. Read to the children about three pages, dealing with the luxury of the Macedonians, Alexander's march to Bactria, and the death of Darius. *"Furthermore, Alexander perceiving on a time that his friends became very dissolute and licentious in diet and life, and that Agnon Teian had his corked shoes nailed with silver nails, that Leonatus also caused divers camels to be laden amongst his carriage with powder of Egypt, to put upon him when he wrestled or used any other exercise of body...he wisely and courteously rebuked them and said: 'I marvel,' said he, 'that you which have fought in so often and great battles, do not remember that they which travail, do sleep more sweet and soundly, than they that take their ease and do nothing...'"*

Read this slowly and distinctly, and *into* the children as much as possible.

Step 4. Ask the children in turn to narrate, each narrating a part of what was read.

Those who have read lesson plans by Mason and her teachers in other subjects, such as Bible lessons, British history, and picture talks, will see examples that can be brought into the Plutarch study as well. For instance, it was common to show pictures (and, in the next example, slide photographs), or to draw a map on the blackboard. Some lessons drew on more than one source, or involved a word-study question or other thinking exercise. It would have been expected that dates and illustrations would be added into the students' Books of Centuries (timeline notebooks).

Another source for information on lessons "as they were taught" is *The Parents' Review*, the periodical that was sent to homes and schools using Charlotte Mason's methods. In his article "A Rational Lesson,"

S. De Brath explains how to begin a lesson.[5]

> ...The clear imaginative realization of a fact may
> proceed by any of the above means [*i.e.* *"questions*
> *judiciously put to bring out what the class already*
> *knows on the subject"*] but perhaps even preferably
> by (4) a picture which will call up familiar and
> kindred ideas; or by repetition (5) of the substance
> of some previous and closely connected lesson
> either in the same, or (6) in an allied branch.
>
> Whatever method be adopted, however, effective
> preparation will have the following essential points:
> —it will arouse and direct the attention, it will make
> clear to the teacher the real ideas already existent in
> the minds of the class, it will cast out the irrelevant
> matter and will link on the new to the old...

De Brath then gives examples of ways to begin, present, and end
lessons in various subject areas, including history. The history example
seems relevant here since it deals with the Roman conquest of Britain.

> Preparation by picture. Show the "Landing of the X.
> Legion," already familiar, and thence recall the
> whole enterprise up to the starting-point of the
> lesson. Five minutes.
>
> Presentation: Show physical map of England,—
> north and west barren and mountainous, south and
> east are fertile plains (they know all this from
> previous geography lessons, and the whole of this
> lesson may be given by questions and narrative,
> mixed). Elicit that the strongest races will keep the
> fertile lands. Caesar's story: three races in Britain—
> Gaels, Hibernians, and Britons, all Celtic (slide,
> Celtic type). Locality of each. Caesar's account,
> recalled from the Latin lessons. Storming of
> Colchester, and the battle against the Silures. The
> Roman roads and the fords of the rivers; why they
> took the directions chosen (slide, Roman Britain,
> map of the roads). Agricola's wall in the north.
> Stations of the Legions at York, Chester, and

Caerleon. Scale distances, and show that as the legion could march thirty miles a day, they could reach any part of the mountain frontier in a week, and fall on flank or rear or any raiders. Detachments throughout the plain country. Conquest complete. Twenty minutes.

Association: ... The summing up of the salient points in each situation is an essential part of the history lesson. A well-known examiner told me not long since of a history teacher of quite exceptional ability in his presentation, who can keep his class white-hot with interest, who is nevertheless unable to make his boys retain the connected history in their minds, so that each successive examination finds them with less and less digested knowledge. The reason was not far to seek; the iron was indeed heated, but the hammer strokes were not given, there was no summary of the essential, and it cooled again nearly into its old form. In our present lesson the essentials are:—The mountains and plains with their properties, the fords of the rivers, the roads, the war sustenance for masses of men, the communication with Gaul, and so with Rome; and the grasp of these is shown by the ability to call up the picture of Roman England, and locate its roads and garrisons on the blank physical map, and say why each was put in the place assigned to it. Five minutes.

This lesson offers several ideas that could be useful for Plutarch, and that we may have seen used in other contexts. For instance, if a legion could cover thirty miles in a day, then it might be interesting to "do the math" on a map of the country, and see how far they could get in a week. The Roman officers would have had to know these things!

Another higher-level thinking skill that appears in De Brath's lesson plan is prediction. If we have rough, barren land on one side, and a fertile plain on the other, which (obviously) do you think the invading force will claim? What will happen to the current occupants? From what you may already know of these groups, which ones would seem to have the advantage in battle (better weapons, strong allies, etc.)?

Finally, De Brath incorporates "Caesar's account, recalled from the Latin lessons." If you know that your students already have special knowledge of a topic, or have read about it in another context, it makes sense to use that previous experience. Maybe you are reading about a part of the world where you have travelled or have family roots; feel free to use those natural connections.

These are just a few ideas to get you started. Enjoy the journey!

Notes

1. Charlotte Mason, *Parents and Children*, pp.231-232.

2. Charlotte Mason, *Home Education*, p.286.

3. *In Memoriam*, Parents' National Educational Union, 1923.

4. Miss M. Ambler, "'Plutarch's Lives' as Affording Some Education as a Citizen," *The Parents' Review*, 12 (1901): 521-527, AmblesideOnline.

5. S. De Brath, "A Rational Lesson." Part One, *The Parents' Review*, 8 (1897): 119-125, AmblesideOnline.
    https://www.amblesideonline.org/PR/PR08p119RationalLesson.shtml

The Life of Publius Valerius Publicola

Introductory Notes

How Do You Pronounce Publicola?

"Publicola" should be pronounced with the stress on the second syllable, as in "ability."

Who was Publicola? When did he live?

In Plutarch's comparison of Publicola and Solon (not included here), he says that Publicola was "the most eminent amongst the Romans" and "the fountain of their honour."

We don't know exactly when Publicola was born; in fact, some modern historians consider him more legendary than factual. However, Plutarch treats the events of his life as history, and, for the purposes of this study, we will do the same.

We can make a guess that Publicola was about forty years old when this story begins, since he was already established as a civic leader; so that would put his birth at around 550 B.C. He might have been even older, as he did not live long after the main events of this story; but it gives us a convenient starting place. At that time, the most powerful king in the world was Cyrus the Great of Persia. Just a few years later, Cyrus made an important decision regarding the Jewish people who had been deported from their homeland and were now under his rule: they would be allowed to return and rebuild the temple in Jerusalem (it was consecrated in 516 B.C.).

Those living in Rome may not have been too aware of events in

Jerusalem, but they surely did know the power of the Persian Empire, especially under Darius the Great (reigned 522 B.C.-486 B.C.). In 512 B.C., just for example, Darius scooped up eastern Thrace, Macedonia, and the Libyan Kingdom. One of the few holdouts against his power was Greece (not the modern nation, but a collection of city-states). The Greeks were about to begin a war of resistance that would lead to the "Golden Age" of Athens. But Italy (fortunately perhaps) was still a bit of a backwater, so it hadn't been noticed much by the Persian superpower.

Publius Valerius Publicola grew up in the city of Rome, in a wealthy family descended from the tribe of the Sabines. He was named for an ancestor who was known for his wisdom and peace-making ability. He himself began earning the citizens' respect even before the main events of this story took place, and it seemed sure that if Rome became a republic, he would be one of its leaders.

Who was Tarquinius (Tarquin)?

Lucius Tarquinius Superbus became king in 534 B.C, and under his rule, Rome became the most powerful of the Latin cities. About the only other positive thing that can be said about this Tarquinius (or Tarquin) is that he began the building of important sites in Rome, such as the Temple of Jupiter. When his son's outrageous behaviour caused a public scandal, a coalition of rebels deposed the Tarquin family.

Who was Brutus?

Another major character is Lucius Junius Brutus, usually called Brutus. He and Valerius (Publicola) headed the revolt against Tarquin, and he was one of the first consuls chosen to lead the new Republic. He was an ancestor of the later Brutus who conspired against Julius Caesar.

What was the Roman Republic?

Many students will have heard of the Roman Empire, but they need to know that it had a five-hundred-years-long predecessor called the Roman Republic, ruled not by an emperor but by elected officials. The word "republic" comes from the same root as *Publicola*, meaning "of the people."

So that no one person would have too much power or be in office for too long, the Romans decided to elect two consuls, or co-rulers, every year. (It is interesting that the date considered as the official beginning of Athenian democracy, 508 B.C., coincides with these events in Rome.)

Who were the Tuscans?

This is a bit confusing, both in language and details. Tuscany was part of a region of Central Italy called Etruria, and the people of that whole region were the Etruscans. The Etruscan civilization had flourished in earlier periods, but by this time it was being absorbed by the surrounding cultures. The word for Etruscans in Latin is *Tusci*, which adds to the confusion. North translates the people as Thuscans and their region as Thuscane; Dryden says Tuscans and Tuscany.

What were Lictors, Axes, Rods, and *Fasces*?

The consuls, or co-rulers, of the Republic had a bodyguard of twelve men, called **lictors**. Each lictor carried a bundle of sticks (**rods**) that also contained an **axe**; the whole thing was called the *fasces* (*fasces* can be singular or plural). Originally this was not just a symbol of power, but a weapon or instrument of official punishment. Later, as you will read in the story, the axes were removed and the *fasces* became more symbolic. Older students who are interested in words may want to explore the connection between *fasces* and "fascism."

Top Vocabulary Terms in the Life of Publicola

If you know these words, you are well on the way to mastering the vocabulary of this *Life*. They will not be repeated in the lessons.

consul: one of two co-rulers in Rome (see note above)

famine: lack of food

13

Forum: the public square and marketplace in Rome, where business and legal matters were conducted

magnanimity: Dryden uses this word to describe Publicola (**Lesson Six**). To be **magnanimous** is to be noble, and to have a generous spirit; **magnanimity** is the noun form.

republic: see note above

Senate: the governing assembly of ancient Rome. During the time of the kings, it functioned mostly as an advisory council (although, interestingly, it did have the power to elect new kings). The Senate held its greatest power during the years of the Republic, and it continued to function (though with less power) through the Empire period, and even afterwards.

suffer: allow, permit

surname: a last name, but not necessarily a family name; it was also called an *agnomen*. "Publicola" is an example of a Roman surname.

tyrant: one who rules with absolute power

usurp: take a position illegally or by force

Lesson One

Introduction (for the teacher)

How did Charlotte Mason begin a new *Life*? She started with something that the students already knew, something that had been studied recently or that could be compared. Maybe you have been reading about the Roman Empire, or about the events leading up to the American War of Independence and the formation of a government afterwards. Or, if all this is fairly new for your student, you can find out what he or she does know about Ancient Rome. If nothing else, you will want to show where Rome is, and talk about the idea of city-states. Rome was a city, not a country, but it had its own government, and later it came to rule other cities and countries as well.

To get things started, you may want to talk about names and nicknames, including Roman-style names. Other than King Tarquin (properly called Lucius Tarquinius Superbus), the first two characters we will be discussing are Publius Valerius Publicola and Lucius Junius Brutus; but they were usually called Valerius (in the beginning) and Brutus. A *cognomen* was a person's first or personal name; his second name showed his family, although he could be referred to by that name (in the same way that we do); and a third name, an *agnomen* or nickname, could be added to distinguish a particular person. You can probably think of more recent examples where people have extra nicknames or titles added; you may even have friends you call "Jim Smith down the street" or "Jim on the basketball team." King Tarquin's *agnomen* meant "the proud." Note that Brutus also had three names, but none of them was an *agnomen*.

That might also lead to a short discussion of the *agnomen* given to Valerius, which was **Publicola**, a man of the people, or loved by the people. Some translators spell that name **Poplicola**, which might give you another clue as to its meaning. What sort of a person would be given that name? (Write down your ideas.)

Vocabulary

Such was Solon: Plutarch's *Life of Solon* comes just before that of *Publicola.*

accession: addition

Romans and Sabines: these two tribes had formerly been at war with each other

eloquence: the ability to speak well and persuasively

liberally: generously, freely

(she killing herself after violence had been done to her): Dryden's translation; North's is less euphemistic.

deposed: removed, "kicked out"

acquiesced: agreed

odious: hateful, repulsive

grateful: appealing, welcome

insolence: arrogance, tyranny

practice of the bar: legal work

gave an occasion of discourse: made people talk

give the test to the Senate upon the altars: require each senator to take a public oath of loyalty

People

Special note: Most of the people in this story are described in the text and do not need further explanation. Later Plutarch studies will make more use of this section.

Lucius Brutus, etc.: see introductory notes

Historic Occasions

Special note: Publicola's story takes place within quite a short time, and several of the early lessons are simply "509 B.C." Later Plutarch studies will make fuller use of this section.

509 BC.: Tarquin deposed; beginning of the Roman Republic

On the Map

By the end of *Publicola*, students should be able to pick out the approximate location of Rome on a map of Italy (where is it on the "boot" shape?). They should also know that it was built on the Tiber River, something that is mentioned in this story. Recognizing the Mediterranean Sea and the Greek peninsula will be useful later on.

It would be useful to find a map of the Roman Empire at its height, and compare it with one from the early days of the Republic (and perhaps also a modern map of Europe). What do you recognize? What is different? In the same way, you might find illustrations of ancient Rome, but note that many of the famous buildings were built in a much later period. For instance, it would be an anachronism to draw Plutarch going to the Colosseum; but the Forum was already an important part of the city.

Where to find such maps? Charlotte Mason suggested using resources such as Dent's *Atlas of Ancient and Classical Geography*, which can be found online. A newer resource is the *Historical Atlas of Ancient Rome* by Nick Constable (Checkmark Books/Thalamus Publishing, 2003). A Bible atlas can often substitute for a more general one. (A handy tip for those needing a quick map reference: look in the backs of Bibles! Maps of Paul's journeys will include Greece, Italy, and the various islands of the Mediterranean. Some Bibles will also include general maps from different time periods.) It is also fairly easy to find appropriate maps online, especially by searching for specific events such as battles.

(Where possible, I have used modern spellings for place names.)

Reading

Such was Solon. To him we compare Publicola, who received this later title from the Roman people for his merit, as a noble **accession** to his former name, Publius Valerius. He descended from Valerius, a man amongst the early citizens, reputed the principle reconciler of the differences betwixt the **Romans and Sabines**, and one that was most instrumental in persuading their kings to assent to peace and union. Thus descended, Publius Valerius, as it is said, whilst Rome remained under its kingly government obtained as great a name from his **eloquence** as from his riches, using the one rightly and freely, for the maintenance of justice, and the other **liberally** and courteously, for the relief of the poor; thereby giving assurance that, should the government fall into a republic, he would become a chief man in the community.

If you have never read Plutarch before, consider stopping to narrate here before you go any further. What do you know so far about Valerius (that is, Publicola)? Why was he held in such esteem by the Romans?

It chanced that King Tarquin, surnamed "the proud," being come to the crown by no good lawful means, but, contrarily, by indirect and wicked ways, and behaving himself not like a king, but like a cruel tyrant: the people much hated and detested him, by reason of the death of Lucretia **(she killing herself after violence had been done to her)**; and so the whole city rose and rebelled against him. **Lucius Brutus** taking upon him to be the head and captain of this insurrection and rebellion, came to Valerius before all others, and, with his zealous assistance, **deposed** the kings.

Stop and narrate if you want.

Now whilst they were thinking that the people would choose someone alone to be chief ruler over them, instead of a king, Valerius **acquiesced**, that to rule was rather Brutus's due, as the author of the democracy. But when the name of monarchy was **odious** to the people, and a divided power appeared more **grateful** in the prospect, and two were chosen to hold it, Valerius entertained hopes that he might be elected consul with Brutus.

Stop and narrate if you want. Why did the Romans think it would be better to have two leaders at once?

Howbeit this hope failed him. For against Brutus's will, Tarquinius Collatinus (the husband of Lucretia) was chosen consul with him: not because he was a man of greater virtue, or of better estimation than Valerius. But the nobles, dreading the return of their kings, who still used all endeavours abroad and solicitations at home, were resolved upon a chieftain of an intense hatred to them [the kings], and noways likely to yield.

Stop and narrate if you want. Why was Tarquinius Collatinus chosen as co-consul with Brutus?

Now, Valerius was troubled that his desire to serve his country should be doubted, because he had sustained no private injury from the **insolence** of the tyrants. He withdrew from the Senate and **practice of the bar**, quitting all public concerns; which **gave an occasion of discourse**, and fear, too, lest his anger should reconcile him to the king's side, and he should prove the ruin of the state, tottering as yet under the uncertainties of a change.

Stop and narrate if you want.

But Brutus [was] doubtful of some others, and determined to **give the test to the Senate upon the altars**. Upon the day appointed, Valerius came with cheerfulness into the Forum, and was the first man that [swore] "in no way to submit or yield to Tarquin's propositions, but rigorously to maintain liberty"; which gave great satisfaction to the Senate, and assurance to the consuls, his action soon after showing the sincerity of his oath.

Narration and Discussion

Special note: As explained in the introduction, you can choose among the discussion questions and activities. It is not necessary to ask every one, or even to use them at all if your students prefer simply to narrate.

Do you think it is significant that Plutarch says Valerius was the first man to take the oath of loyalty? What does it say about his character?

What might Valerius have done (as the people feared) if he had been of a spiteful nature?

For further thought: Think about well-known names in history. What it would mean to you to be named for a famous ancestor? Do you think it is more important to be respected because of your family or because of your own actions? (Look up Proverbs 22:1.)

Creative Narration: If you would like to extend this lesson, it could be dramatized in some form (including news interviews).

Word Study

*Special note: **Word Study** was included in the first version of the Plutarch Primer, but was dropped in later volumes. I have kept these notes in the revised version, however; they may be "rabbit trails," but interesting ones nonetheless.*

Eloquence: the ability to use language with elegance, force, and accuracy. *Loqui* is Latin for "talk." What does **loquacious** mean?

Lesson Two

Introduction

Special note: The Introduction sections from this point on are written for the students. The teacher can read them, or incorporate the ideas into review of previous lessons, introduction of a new word or place on the map, etc.

If you were the head of the new Roman government, how would you feel about receiving a "friendly" visit from agents of the former king? Would you even let them in the door? Tarquin promised that he would be a nicer king in the future if the Romans asked him to return, but threatened that if they did not, he would come back by force.

Special Note on Family Names

Although Plutarch wrote in Greek, names of Roman families and individuals are often given in Latin format. In Latin, plurals are created by changing the ending of a word (or name) to "i," even when the root word already ends in "i." In this lesson we hear about the Aquillian family, which in its proper plural is the Aquillii; and the Vitellian family, whose members are the Vitellii. However, these are hard to spell and pronounce. Therefore, though it is not completely accurate to the text, this version will refer to them as the Aquillians and the Vitellians. You're welcome.

Vocabulary

> **sweet and lowly speeches:** Dryden translates this "popular and specious proposals"; specious means farfetched or untrue, which isn't exactly the same as lowly, but you get the idea.

> **to dulce and soften the hardened hearts of the multitude:** To **dulce** is to sweeten and soothe. Dryden: "to seduce the people."

nought but: nothing but

peril: endanger

occasion of new stir: further upheaval

wherewithal to keep them: enough to live on

a fast and resolute man: Dryden translates this "a man of vehement and unbending nature," and this is important to remember about Brutus.

so much as subsistence in exile: Brutus was not in favour of providing even a living allowance to those who had been exiled

a private man: a private citizen, not holding public office

eminent: well-known and respected

seduced: lured, enticed

emancipation: freedom

imbecility: mental incapacity; slowness of wits. North says that Brutus "had feigned himself mad." He had allowed himself to seem foolish or incapable in some way, probably as protection.

a murdered man: it is not clear where they were supposed to find one

People, Historic Occasions, On the Map

As there are no extra entries for these, these sections will be skipped for this lesson. This might be an opportunity to review mapwork etc. from previous lessons.

Reading

For there came ambassadors to Rome which brought letters from King Tarquin, full of **sweet and lowly speeches** to win the favour of the people, with commission to use all the mildest means they could, **to dulce and soften the hardened hearts of the multitude**: who declared how the king had left all pride and cruelty, and meant to ask **nought but** reasonable things.

21

Stop and narrate if you want.

The consuls thought best to give them open audience, and to suffer them to speak to the people. But Valerius was against it, declaring it might **peril** the state much, and deliver **occasion of new stir** unto a multitude of poor people, which were more afraid of wars than of tyranny.

After that, there came other ambassadors also, which said that Tarquin would from thenceforth forever give over and renounce his title to the kingdom, and [also his intention] to make any more wars, but besought them only, that they would at the least deliver him and his friends their money and goods, that they might have **wherewithal to keep them** in their banishment. Now, several inclining to the request, and Collatinus in particular favouring it, Brutus, **a fast and resolute man**, rushed into the Forum, there proclaiming his fellow-consul to be a traitor, in granting subsidies to tyranny, and supplies for a war to those to whom it was monstrous to allow **so much as subsistence in exile**.

Stop and narrate if you want.

This caused an assembly of the citizens, amongst whom the first that spoke was Caius Minucius, **a private man**, who advised Brutus, and urged the Romans to keep the property, and employ it *against* the tyrants, rather than to remit it *to* the tyrants, to be used against themselves. Notwithstanding, the Romans were of opinion that, having gotten the liberty for which they fought with the tyrants, they should not disappoint the offered peace by keeping back their goods, but rather they should throw their goods out after them.

Stop and narrate if you want.

The question, however, of his property was the least part of Tarquin's design; the demand sounded the feelings of the people, and was preparatory to a conspiracy which the ambassadors endeavoured to excite. [For this reason they delayed] their return, under pretence of selling some of the goods and reserving others to be sent away; till, in fine, they corrupted two of the most **eminent** families in Rome: the Aquillian family, which had three [senators], and the Vitellian family, which had two.

Stop and narrate if you want. What was the real purpose of the ambassadors' remaining in Rome?

Those all were, by the mother's side, nephews to Collatinus; besides which, Brutus had a special alliance to the Vitellians from his marriage with their sister, by whom he had several children; two of whom, of their own age, their near relations and daily companions, the Vitellians **seduced** to join in the plot, to ally themselves to the great house and royal hopes of the Tarquins, and gain **emancipation** from the "violence and **imbecility**" of their father, whose austerity to offenders they termed "violence"; while the "imbecility" which he had long feigned, to protect himself from the tyrants, still it appears, was, in name at least, ascribed to him.

Stop and narrate if you want. Why were the two sons of Brutus so willing to join the supporters of Tarquin?

Upon these considerations the youths came to confer with the Aquillians, and thought it convenient to bind themselves with a great and horrible oath, drinking the blood of **a murdered man**, and touching his entrails. For which design they met at the house of the Aquillians. The building chosen for the transaction was, as was natural, dark and unfrequented; and a slave named Vindicius had, as it chanced, concealed himself there, not out of design or any intelligence of the affair, but, accidentally being within, seeing with how much haste and concern they came in, he was afraid to be discovered, and placed himself behind a chest, where he was able to observe their actions and overhear their debates.

Their resolutions were to kill the consuls, and they wrote letters to Tarquin to this effect, and gave them to the ambassadors, who were lodging upon the spot with the Aquillians, and were present at the consultation.

Narration and Discussion

Valerius/Publicola was not one of the consuls, yet the Romans listened to his opinion on allowing Tarquin's ambassadors to speak publicly. Why do you think they respected his wisdom on this? What do you think might have happened if the men had been allowed to speak?

Why do you think Plutarch says that the poorer people "were more afraid of wars than of tyranny?"

If you were the ambassadors, what sort of people would you try to lure onto your hook? Why do you think they would have been especially delighted with these particular young men? Read Proverbs 1:10–33. How could this passage help someone avoid making a similar mistake?

Creative Narration: An obvious extension of this lesson might be to act parts of it out. Another option might be to write a letter from one character to another.

Word Study

In the vocabulary list, we have "'To **dulce** is to sweeten and soothe." **Dulce** is an uncommon word in English; but we do use **dulcet**, meaning gentle and melodious. For fun: find out the meaning of "dulce de leche" or "carbón dulce."

Lesson Three

Introduction

The slave Vindicius had overheard a plot to assassinate the consuls Brutus and Collatinus. He did not want to go directly to either of them, because he feared to bring such a great charge against close family members of the consuls. In the end, he decided to go to the one person he knew who was wise, powerful and also kind—Valerius. Valerius acted promptly to seize both the traitors and the incriminating papers,

24

and justice was carried out swiftly.

This section is not for the faint of heart. It shows the consequence of the treachery of Brutus' sons, and the importance that the Republic held in the eyes of their father and others such as Valerius/Publicola.

Vocabulary

quitted: left

indigences of humble people: needs of the poor

made a complete discovery to him: told him everything

in the goods: among the things that were to be sent back to the king

bondman: slave

they should banish them: that is, instead of having them put to death

held his peace: said nothing

indictment: accusation

austere: stern

People

Romulus: the legendary founder of Rome

Historic Occasions

509 B.C.: Death of Brutus's sons

Reading

From this point on the narration breaks will not be marked, but you may wish to go through the text ahead of time and mark good stopping points. Some students prefer to listen to longer passages before narrating; others need to pause and recap more frequently.

Upon their departure, Vindicius secretly **quitted** the house, but was at a loss what to do in the matter. For he thought it dangerous (as it was indeed) to go and accuse the two sons unto the father (which was Brutus) of so wicked and detestable a treason; and the nephews unto their uncle, which was Collatinus; yet he knew no private Roman to whom he could intrust secrets of such importance. Unable, however, to keep silence, and burdened with his knowledge, he went and addressed himself to Valerius, whose known freedom and kindness of temper were an inducement; as he was a person to whom the needy had easy access, and who never shut his gates against the petitions or **indigences of humble people**. But when Vindicius came and **made a complete discovery to him**, his brother Marcus and his own wife being present, Valerius was struck with amazement, and by no means would dismiss the discoverer, but confined him to the room, and placed his wife as a guard to the door, sending his brother in the interim to beset the king's palace, and seize, if possible, the writings there, and to see that none of their servants fled.

Valerius, being followed (according to his manner) with a great train of his friends and people that waited on him, went straight unto the house of the Aquillians, who by chance were absent from home; and so, forcing an entrance through the gates, they lit upon the letters then lying in the lodgings of the ambassadors.

Meanwhile the Aquillians returned in all haste, and, coming to blows about the gate, endeavoured a recovery of the letters. The other party made a resistance, and throwing their gowns around their opponents' necks, at last, after much struggling on both sides, made their way with their prisoners through the streets into the Forum. The like engagement happened about the king's palace, where Marcus seized some other letters which it was designed should be conveyed away **in the goods**, and, laying hands on such of the king's people as he could find, dragged them also into the Forum.

There the consuls having caused silence to be made, Valerius sent to his house for this **bondman** Vindicius, to be brought before the consuls; then the traitors were openly accused, and their letters read, and they had not the face to answer one word. All that were present, being amazed, hung down their heads, and beheld the ground, and not a man [dared] once open his mouth to speak, excepting a few, who, to gratify Brutus, began to say that **they should [only] banish them**;

and Collatinus also gave them some hope, because he fell to weeping; and Valerius in like manner, [because] he **held his peace**.

But Brutus, calling his two sons by their names, "Canst not thou," said he, "O Titus, or thou, Tiberius, make any defense against the **indictment?**" The question being thrice proposed, and no reply made, he turned himself to the lictors and cried, "They are now in your hands, do justice." *[Dryden: "What remains is your duty."]*

So soon as he had spoken these words, the sergeants laid hold immediately upon the two young men, and tearing their clothes off their backs, bound their hands behind them, and then whipped them with rods: which was such a pitiful sight to all the people, that they could not find in their hearts to behold it, but turned themselves another way, because they would not see it. But contrariwise, they say that their own father had never his eye off them, neither did change his **austere** and fierce countenance, with any pity or natural affection towards them, but steadfastly did behold the punishment of his own children, until they were laid flat on the ground, and both their heads stricken off with an axe before him. He then departed, committing the rest to the judgement of his colleague.

This was such an act, as men cannot sufficiently praise nor reprove enough. For either it was his excellent virtue that made his mind so quiet, or else the greatness of his misery that took away the feeling of his sorrow: whereof neither the one nor the other was any small matter, but passing the common nature of man, that hath in it both divineness, and sometime beastly brutishness. But it is better the judgement of men should commend his fame, than that the affection of men by their judgements should diminish his virtue. For the Romans hold opinion, that Brutus did a greater work in the establishment of the government than **Romulus** [did] in the foundation of the city.

Narration and Discussion

In his story of a later Brutus (the one involved in the assassination of Julius Caesar), Plutarch describes the first Brutus this way:

> But that ancient Brutus was of a severe and
> inflexible nature, like steel of too hard a temper,
> and having never had his character softened by
> study and thought, he let himself be so far

> transported with his rage and hatred against
> tyrants, that, for conspiring with them, he
> proceeded to the execution even of his own sons.

Was it fanatical rage and hatred that allowed Brutus to carry out this deed? Or was it a necessary (and courageous) act of justice?

Creative Narration: In spite of the execution scene, this section has several interesting and enjoyable moments. News interviews, newspaper stories, or one character telling another what happened might all work well.

Creative Narration (for older students): The dilemma of the slave Vindicius, who overheard everything and had to decide what to do with his information, is worthy of a Shakespearean monologue. In fact, Plutarch was one of Shakespeare's favorite books, and he borrowed heavily from the *Lives* for several of his plays. Pretend you are Shakespeare looking for new play material, and write the conspiracy scene (and/or Vindicius's musings afterward) in dramatic form.

For further thought: Explain this sentence: "For the Romans hold opinion, that Brutus did a greater work in the establishment of the government than **Romulus** [did] in the foundation of the city."

For further thought (for older students): A Biblical parallel to Brutus may be found in II Samuel 19:1-8. When David mourned excessively for his son Absalom, General Joab came to him and reproved him, saying that David was ignoring all his other subjects who had fought for him. David listened to Joab's wisdom, and went out and "sat in the gate" where he belonged. Do you agree that it is the mark of a true leader to put his personal needs and feelings aside for the sake of his people?

Lesson Four

Introduction

Because Vindicius, the star witness, was the slave of the Aquillians, the defendants in this court case, they requested permission to have him given into their own custody (and they would therefore have prevented him from testifying against them). Collatinus was more than happy to agree to this (not wanting to see his nephews executed), but Valerius stepped in and demanded protection for Vindicius and punishment for the traitors. His reputation for justice and fairness was finally rewarded.

Vocabulary

consternation: dismay

easiness and tardiness: this is Dryden's phrase. North says that the accused relaxed somewhat when they "saw the other consul proceed gently and mildly against them."

some women: relatives of the accused, and likely also of Collatinus

relinquished his charge: gave up his position as consul

in his room: in his place

tribe: clan, family

razed: demolished

commit them to the flail: finish harvesting them

ford: crossing place

Historic Occasions

509 B.C.: Publicola elected co-consul after the abdication of Collatinus

Reading

Part One

Upon Brutus's departure out of the Forum, **consternation**, horror, and silence for some time possessed all that reflected on what was done; the **easiness and tardiness**, however, of Collatinus gave confidence to the Aquillians to request some time to answer their charge, and that Vindicius, their servant, should be remitted into their hands and no longer harboured amongst their accusers. The consul seemed inclined to their proposal, and was proceeding to break up the assembly; but Valerius would not suffer Vindicius, who was surrounded by his people, to be surrendered, nor the meeting to withdraw without punishing the traitors; and at length laid violent hands upon the Aquillians, and, calling Brutus to his assistance, exclaimed against the unreasonable course of Collatinus, to impose upon his colleague [Brutus] the necessity of taking away the lives of his own sons, and yet have thoughts of gratifying **some women** with the lives of traitors and public enemies.

Collatinus, displeased at this, and commanding Vindicius to be taken away, the lictors made their way through the crowd and seized their man, and struck all who endeavoured a rescue. Valerius's friends headed the resistance, and the people cried out for Brutus, who, returning, on silence being made, told them:

> For mine own children, I alone have been their
> sufficient judge, to see them have the law according
> to their deservings: the rest I have left freely to the
> judgement of the people. Wherefore (said he), if any
> man be disposed to speak, let him stand up, and
> persuade the people as he thinketh best.

Then there needed no more words, but only to hearken what the people cried: who with one voice and consent condemned them, and cried execution, and accordingly they had their heads stricken off.

Part Two

Now the consul Collatinus long before [had been viewed] in some suspicion, as allied to the kings, and disliked for his surname, because he was called "Tarquinius"; but after this had happened, perceiving himself an offence to everyone, he **relinquished his charge** and departed from the city.

At the new elections **in his room,** Valerius obtained, with high honour, the consulship, as a just reward of his zeal; of which he thought Vindicius deserved a share, whom he made, first of all freedmen, a citizen of Rome, and gave him the privilege of voting in what **tribe** soever he was pleased to be enrolled *[brief omission]*.

These things thus passed over, the goods of the kings were given to the spoil of the people, and their palaces were **razed** and overthrown.

Part Three

The pleasantest part of the Field of Mars, which Tarquin had owned, was devoted to the service of that god; but, it happening to be harvest season, and the sheaves yet being on the ground, they thought it not proper to **commit them to the flail**, or unsanctify them with any use; and, therefore, carrying them to the river-side, and trees withal that were cut down, they cast all into the water, to the end that the field being dedicated to the god Mars, should be left bare, without bearing any fruit at all.

These sheaves, thus thrown into the river, were carried down by the stream not far from thence, unto a **ford** and shallow place of the water, where they first did stay, and did let the other which came after, that it could go no further: there these heaps gathered together, and lay so close one to another, that they began to sink and settle fast in the water. Afterwards the stream of the river brought down continually such mud and gravel, that it ever increased the heap of corn more and more in such sort, that the force of the water could no more remove it from thence, but rather softly pressing and driving it together, did firm and harden it, and made it grow so to land. Thus this heap rising still in greatness and firmness, by reason that all that came down the river stayed there, it grew in the end, and by time to spread so far, that at this day it is called the "Holy Island" in Rome.

[short omission for length]

Narration and Discussion

Why do you think Valerius/Publicola cared about the fate of one very lowly slave (more than he did about the lives of two Roman citizens)?

What character qualities did he show in this passage?

31

Why didn't Tarquin receive the goods that had been packed up to be sent to him? What happened to them? Why was the grain from his field dumped into the water? Can you think of any reasons why the two types of things were not treated in the same way?

Creative Narration: Describe these events from the point of view of Vindicius.

Find Out More: What did it mean to be a citizen of Rome (as Vindicius now was)? Who could be a citizen? What rights did a citizen have? St. Paul was a citizen of Rome; how did his citizenship help him on at least one occasion?

Lesson Five

Introduction

A very short lesson about revenge, battles, scary things, and the first-ever Roman Triumph.

Vocabulary

succour: help

levied: gathered

made their rendezvous: met to fight

fell together: were both killed

onset: beginning

conjecture: guessing, speculating

plundered: looted

triumphed: was given a ceremonial parade through Rome

People

Tuscans: see the note in the introduction

Historic Occasions

Early 509 B.C.: Death of Brutus at the battle of Silva Arsia

March 1, 509 BC.: Triumph of Valerius

Reading

Part One

Tarquinius then being past hope of ever entering into his kingdom again, went yet unto the **Tuscans** for **succour**, which were very glad of him; and so they **levied** a great army together, hoping to have put him in his kingdom again. The consuls headed the Romans against them, and **made their rendezvous** in certain holy places, the one called the Arsian Grove, the other the Aesuvian Meadow.

When they came into action, Aruns the son of Tarquin, and Brutus the Roman consul, encountering each other not accidentally, but out of hatred and rage, the one to avenge tyranny and enmity to his country, the other his banishment, set spurs to their horses, and, engaging with more fury than forethought, disregarding their own security, **fell together** in the combat. This dreadful **onset** was hardly followed by a more favourable end: both armies, doing and receiving equal damage, were separated by a storm.

Part Two

Valerius was much concerned, not knowing what the result of the day was, and seeing his men as well dismayed at the sight of their own dead, as rejoiced at the loss of the enemy; so apparently equal in the number was the slaughter on either side. Each party, however, felt surer of defeat from the actual sight of their own dead, than they could feel of victory from **conjecture** about those of their adversaries.

The night being come (and such as one may presume must follow such a battle), and the armies laid to rest, they say that the grove shook, and uttered a voice, saying that the Tuscans had lost one man more than the Romans; clearly a divine announcement; and the Romans at once received it with shouts and expressions of joy; whilst the Tuscans, through fear and amazement, deserted their tents, and were for the most part dispersed.

The Romans, falling upon the remainder [of the Tuscans], amounting to nearly five thousand, took them prisoners, and **plundered** the camp; when they numbered the dead, they found on the Tuscans' side eleven thousand and three hundred, exceeding their own loss but by one man.

This battle was fought (as they say) the last day of February, and the consul Valerius **triumphed** in honour of it, being the first of the consuls that ever entered into Rome triumphing upon a chariot drawn with four horses, which sight the people found honourable and goodly to behold, and were not offended withal (as some seem to report) nor yet did envy him for that he began it. For if it had been so, that custom had not been followed with so good acceptation, nor had continued so many years as it did afterwards.

Narration and Discussion

The question of the "divine announcement" may be the first thing to discuss here. It is obvious that *something* happened; somehow the Roman troops received a much-needed boost of confidence that allowed them to jump up and plunder the Tuscan tents. We might think that it was the sudden shouting and rush of soldiers that frightened the Tuscans away, but Plutarch seems to be saying that the Tuscans also heard the voice; that is, that they ran away before the Romans attacked their camp. Is there any other logical explanation for what happened? Is it possible that it was some kind of trick?

Plutarch says that Brutus and Tarquin's son both acted "with more fury than reason." Was this self-sacrifice the best choice, or would Brutus have done better by leading his men in the rest of the battle?

Finally, look at the role of Valerius/Publicola in this battle. True to what we know of his steady leadership, he was not out for personal revenge, but continued to do his best even when the army seemed to be defeated. Afterwards, he continued to grow in public esteem, including becoming (according to Plutarch) the first consul ever to be given a triumph. Why do you think he was greeted with so much enthusiasm, or (to put it another way) so little "envy?"

Creative Narration: Choose a scene from the reading to illustrate; or write a series of headlines that might have appeared in the "Rome Daily News."

Find Out More: Find out more about Roman triumphs. What typically happened when a hero entered the city? Share what you have learned in some creative format.

Word Study

Conjecture: to put forth a theory; guess, suppose, speculate. The word comes from a Middle French verb, *jacere*, to throw. To **conjecture** is to throw a conclusion together. **Project** comes from the same root, and means to throw forward (or extend). What do you think the literal meaning of **interject** might be?

Lesson Six

Introduction

This reading describes political and legal changes that Valerius/Publicola made while he still had absolute power, temporary though it might be. Pay particular attention to the ways that Publicola (he was finally called by that name) showed **magnanimity**.

Vocabulary

obsequies: funeral rites

funeral oration: speech, eulogy

commendation: praise

verbal harangues: speeches

ill to come to it: awkward to access it

it was a marvellous pomp and state: it created a splendid display

contended not: didn't argue about it

magnanimity: generosity of spirit (see **Top Vocabulary Terms**)

Vica Pota: a Roman goddess, possibly of victory

he put away the carrying of the axes from the rods: from now on, the rods would be carried without the axes, as symbols of the government's power but not used as weapons or for punishment

embase his dignity and greatness: lower his own dignity

sue for the consulship: seek election as consul

thwart: prevent, block

usurp any magistracy: seize any government position

no more custom, nor any impost whatsoever: no more taxes

the commonalty: the working class, also called the *plebeians*

obol: a Greek coin. Perhaps Plutarch was trying to use a term that would be familiar to his readers (since, as he says, the use of coins was uncommon in the early Republic).

Reading

Part One

The people applauded likewise also the honours he did to his fellow consul Brutus, in adding to his **obsequies** a **funeral oration**, which was so much liked by the Romans, and found so good a reception, that it became customary for the best men to celebrate the funerals of great citizens with speeches in their **commendation** *[omission for length]*. But

36

they did most envy Valerius, and bear him grudge, because Brutus (whom the people did acknowledge for father of their liberty) had not presumed to rule without a colleague, but united one and then another to him in his commission; while Valerius, they said, centering all authority in himself, seemed not in any sense a successor to Brutus in the consulship, but to Tarquin in the tyranny; he might make **verbal harangues** to Brutus's memory, yet, when he was attended with all the rods and axes, proceeding down from a house than which the king's house that he had demolished had not been statelier, those actions showed him an imitator of Tarquin.

And to say truly, Valerius dwelt in a house a little too sumptuously built and seated, upon the hanging of the hill called Mount Velia: and because it stood high, it overlooked all the marketplace, so that any man might easily see from thence what was done there. Furthermore, it was very **ill to come to it**; but when he came out of his house, **it was a marvellous pomp and state** to see him come down from so high a place, and with a train after him, that carried the majesty of a king's court.

But Valerius showed how well it were for men in power and great offices to have ears that give admittance to truth before flattery; for upon his friends telling him that he displeased the people, he **contended not**, neither resented it, but while it was still night, sending for a number of work-people, pulled down his house and levelled it with the ground.

Insomuch as the next day following, when the Romans were gathered together in the marketplace, and saw this great sudden ruin, they expressed their wonder and their respect for his **magnanimity**; and their sorrow, as though it had been a human being, for the large and beautiful house which was thus lost to them by an unfounded jealousy; while its owner, their consul, without a roof of his own, had to beg a lodging with his friends. For his friends received him, till a place the people gave him was furnished with a house, though less stately than his own, where now stands the temple, as it is called, of **Vica Pota**.

Part Two

Now because he would not only reform his person, but the office of his consulship, and also would frame himself to the good acceptation and liking of the people: where before he seemed unto them to be fearful, **he put away the carrying of the axes from the rods**, which the sergeants used to bear before the consul. Moreover when he came into the marketplace, where the people were assembled, he caused the rods to be borne downwards, as in token of reverence of the sovereign majesty of the people: which all the magistrates observe yet at this day. Now in all this humble show and lowliness of his, he did not so much **embase his dignity and greatness**, which the common people thought him to have at the first: as he did thereby cut [their] envy from him, winning again as much true authority, as in semblance he would seem to have lost. For this made the people more willing to obey, and readier to submit themselves unto him: insomuch as upon this occasion he was surnamed Publicola, as much to say, as "the people pleaser" [Dryden: "people-lover"]. Which surname he kept ever after, and we from henceforth also writing the rest of his life, will use no other name.

Part Three

He gave free leave to any to **sue for the consulship**. But, not knowing what kind of man they would join fellow consul with him; and fearing lest, through envy or ignorance, the party might **thwart** his purpose and meaning; he employed his sole power and authority, whilst he ruled alone, upon high and noble attempts.

First, he supplied the vacancies of the senators, whom either Tarquin long before had put to death, or the war lately cut off; those that he enrolled, they write, amounted to a hundred and sixty-four. Afterwards he made several laws which added much to the people's liberty, in particular one granting offenders the liberty of appealing to the people from the judgment of the consuls; a second, that made it death to **usurp any magistracy** without the people's consent.

The third was, and all in favour of the poor, that the poor citizens of Rome should pay **no more custom, nor any impost whatsoever**. This made every man the more willing to give himself to some craft or occupation, when he saw his travail should not be taxed, nor taken from him.

Another [law was] against disobedience to the consuls, which was no less popular than the rest, and rather to the benefit of **the commonalty** than to the advantage of the nobles, for it imposed upon disobedience the penalty of ten oxen and two sheep; the price of a sheep being ten **obols**, of an ox, a hundred. For the use of money was then infrequent amongst the Romans, but their wealth in cattle great; even now pieces of property are called *peculia*, from *pecus*, cattle. And in the old time the stamp upon their money was an ox, a sheep, or a hog; and some of them surnamed their sons Suillii, Bubulci, Caprarii, and Porcii, from *caprae*, goats, and *porci*, hogs.

Narration and Discussion

What might have happened at this point if Publicola had allowed himself to give in to selfish ambition? How did he make it clear that he had no such intentions?

Why was one of Publicola's first moves to increase the number of senators? Wouldn't this weaken his own power? Do you think that his tax cuts and other reforms were just ways to gain votes and popularity?

Creative Narration: The story of Publicola having his house torn down lends itself to various creative formats: dramatic presentation, interviews, newscasts, diary entries, even political cartoons.

Lesson Seven

Introduction

This reading can be divided into two parts. The first describes more of Publicola's acts as consul, and the events around the selection of his "co-consuls"—first Lucretius, then Marcus Horatius.

The second part of the reading moves back to Tarquin, who was preparing, with the Tuscans, to attack Rome again. As king, he had designed an ornamental chariot that was supposed to be placed on top of a temple in the Capitol, and he had hired Tuscan craftsmen to complete the work. But who now owned the chariot?

Vocabulary

aspired to a tyranny: planned to become the sole ruler

he gave a licence...: Publicola's new law allowed the "emergency arrest" of anyone suspected of plotting to seize government power.

precedence: the first or "senior" position

portent: omen, supernatural sign

set in a furnace: built a kiln (oven) to fire (bake) it

to subside and be condensed...: Clay normally shrinks (not expands) when it is baked.

soothsayers: those who predict the future, e.g. by interpreting omens

a celestial token from above: a sign from the gods

upon no apparent occasion: for no observable reason

People

Lucretius: Spurius Lucretius Tricipitinus

Marcus Horatius: Marcus Horatius Pulvillus, consul in 509 B.C. (following the death of Lucretius) and again in 507 B.C.

On the Map

Tuscany: a region of central Italy, then called Etruria. (Etruria covered present-day Tuscany but also some other regions.) **Veii** was an important city of Etruria.

Reading

Part One

Amidst this mildness and moderation, for one excessive fault Publicola instituted one excessive punishment: for he made it lawful without trial

40

to take away any man's life that **aspired to a tyranny**, and **acquitted** the slayer, if he produced evidence of the crime. For though it was not probably for a man, whose designs were so great, to escape all notice; yet because it was possible he might, although observed, by force anticipate judgment, which the usurpation itself would then preclude, **he gave a licence to any to anticipate the usurper**.

They greatly commended him also for the law that he made touching the treasury; for because it was necessary for the citizens to contribute out of their estates to the maintenance of wars, and [because] he was unwilling himself to be concerned in the care of it, or to permit his friends, or indeed to let the public money pass into any private house, he did ordain that Saturn's Temple should be the treasury thereof. This order they keep to this present day. Furthermore, he granted the people to choose two young men *quaestors* of the same, as you would say "the treasurers," to take the charge of this money. The two first which were chosen were Publius Veturius and Marcus Minucius, who gathered great sums of money together; for they assessed one hundred and thirty thousand [people], excusing orphans and widows from the payment.

After he had established all these things, he caused **Lucretius**, the father of Lucretia [**Lesson One**] to be chosen fellow consul with him, and gave him the **precedence** in the government, by resigning the *fasces* to him, as due to his years (which privilege of seniority continued to our time). But within a few days Lucretius died, and in a new election **Marcus Horatius** succeeded in that honour, and continued consul for the remainder of the year.

Part Two

Now, whilst Tarquin was making preparations in **Tuscany** for a second war against the Romans, it is said a great **portent** occurred. When Tarquin was king, and had all but completed the buildings of the Capitol, designing, whether from oracular advice or his own pleasure, to erect an earthen chariot upon the top, he entrusted the workmanship to Tuscans of the city **Veii**, but soon after lost his kingdom. The work thus modelled, the Tuscans **set in a furnace**, but the clay showed not those passive qualities which usually attend its nature, **to subside and be condensed upon the evaporation of the**

moisture, but [it] rose and swelled out to that bulk, that, when solid and firm, notwithstanding the removal of the roof and opening the walls of the furnace, it could not be taken out without much difficulty.

The **soothsayers** did expound this, that it was **a celestial token from above,** and promised great prosperity and increase of power unto those that should possess this coach. Whereupon the Tuscans resolved not to deliver it unto the Romans that demanded it, but answered that it did belong unto King Tarquin, and not unto those that had banished him.

A few days after, they had a horserace there [in Veii], with the usual shows and solemnities, and as the charioteer with his garland on his head was quietly driving the victorious chariot out of the ring, the horses, **upon no apparent occasion**, taking fright, either by divine instigation or by accident, hurried away their driver at full speed to Rome; neither did his holding them in prevail, nor his voice, but he was forced along with violence [until], coming to the Capitol, he was thrown out by the gate called *Ratumena*.

This occurrence raised wonder and fear in the Veientines, who now permitted the delivery of the chariot.

Narration and Discussion

Consider the laws that Publicola made, and also his attitudes towards his co-consuls. What do these things show about his character and about his vision for the Roman Republic? (For further thought: How did Publicola's attitude towards holding the treasury money differ from that of Judas Iscariot? (John 12:6))

The second part is the story of Tarquin's chariot. Why do you think the Romans believed so strongly in superstition, omens, and lucky charms? Is there any logical explanation for something which expands rather than shrinks when it is fired? Or is it possible that this part of the story is only legend?

Creative narration: Write or act out a dialogue between imaginary Romans of the time; this could also be a news interview, possibly a "voices on the street" feature. Have them ask this question: To what do you attribute Publicola's success as a leader? Supernatural help (from God or the gods)? His own character and ability? Lucky circumstances and timing? A combination of these?

For further thought: It is said that "power corrupts." Think of rulers (real or fictional) who became greedy or ruthless as their power grew. Can you think of anyone who resisted that temptation?

Lesson Eight

Introduction

With some people, you can't win: even if you deserve all the credit and honour you receive, they won't admit you've earned it, or they'll think you've already got too much. In this section, we see some envy of Publicola creeping in, especially of his having the honour of dedicating the Temple of Jupiter.

The rest of this section tells how the temple was destroyed and rebuilt (which explains why there are no photographs of the Capitol with Tarquin's terracotta chariot on top).

Vocabulary

> **Temple of the Capitoline Jupiter:** a large temple in Rome. As noted below, it was destroyed and rebuilt several times. Parts of the fourth temple can still be viewed in Rome.

> **egg:** urge, encourage

> **make suit for the same:** request that he be in charge of the dedication

> **procured:** managed, arranged

> **intimate some ground for this conjecture:** suggest that this was true

> **discomposed:** bothered

> **in the civil wars; Vitellian sedition:** see **Historic Occasions**

> **not discharge:** not be enough to pay for

talent: a large amount of gold or silver

People

Tarquin the son of Demaratus: the fifth king of Rome

[Lucius] Tarquinius Superbus: the seventh and last king of Rome

Sulla: Roman general and dictator (138-78 B.C.)

Catulus: Quintus Lutatius Catulus Capitolinus, consul in 78 B.C.

Domitian: Emperor from 81 to 96 A.D.; son of **Vespasian** (Emperor from 69 to 79 A.D.)

Historic Occasions

509 B.C.: Dedication of the first Temple of Jupiter

83-82 B.C.: Roman civil wars; destruction of the first temple

69 A.D.: "Year of the Four Emperors"/ Vitellian sedition

69 A.D.: Dedication and destruction of the second temple

75 A.D.: Dedication of the third temple

80 A.D.: Destruction of the third temple

82 A.D.: Fourth temple completed.

392 A.D.: Pagan temples closed by Emperor Theodosius I

Reading

Part One

The building of the **Temple of the Capitoline Jupiter** had been vowed by **Tarquin the son of Demaratus**, when warring with the Sabines. **[Lucius]Tarquinius Superbus**, his son or grandson, built [it], but could not dedicate it, because he lost his kingdom before it was

44

quite finished. And now that it was completed with all its ornaments, Publicola was ambitious to dedicate it. But the noblemen and senators envying his glory, being very angry that he could not content himself with all those honours that he had received in peace, for the good laws he had made, and in wars for the victories he had obtained and well deserved, but further that he would seek the honour of this dedication, which nothing did pertain unto him: they then did **egg** Horatius, and persuaded him to **make suit for the same**.

Occasion fell out at that time, that Publicola must have the leading of the Romans' army into the field. In the meantime, while Publicola was absent, it was **procured** that the people gave their voices to Horatius to consecrate the temple, knowing they could not so well have brought it to pass, he [Publicola] being present.

Others say the consuls drew lots between them, and that it lighted upon Publicola to lead the army against his will, and upon Horatius to consecrate this temple; and what happened in the performance seems to **intimate some ground for this conjecture**. For, upon the Ides of September, which happens about the full moon of the month *Metagitnion*, the people having assembled at the Capitol and silence being enjoined, Horatius, after the performance of other ceremonies, holding the doors, according to custom, was proceeding to pronounce the words of dedication, when Marcus, the brother of Publicola, who had got a place on purpose beforehand near the door, observing his opportunity, cried, "O consul, thy son lies dead in the camp"; which made a great impression upon all others who heard it, yet it nowise **discomposed** Horatius, who returned merely the reply, "Cast the dead out whither you please; I am nor a mourner"; and so [he] completed the dedication. The news was not true, but Marcus thought the lie might avert him from his performance; but it argues him [Horatius] a man of wonderful self-possession, whether he at once saw through the cheat, or, believing it as true, showed no discomposure.

Part Two

The same fortune attended the dedication of the second temple; the first, as has been said, was built by Tarquin, and dedicated by Horatius; it was burnt down **in the civil wars**. The second, **Sulla** built, and dying before the dedication, left that honour to **Catulus**; and when this was demolished in the **Vitellian sedition**, **Vespasian**, with the same success that attended him in other things, began a third and lived to see it finished, but did not live to see it again destroyed, as it presently was; but was as fortunate in dying before its destruction, as Sulla was the reverse in dying before the dedication of his. For immediately after Vespasian's death it was consumed by fire. *[Dryden's addition: The fourth, which now exists, was both built and dedicated by **Domitian**.]*

It is said Tarquin expended forty thousand pounds of silver in the very foundations; but the whole wealth of the richest private man in Rome would **not discharge** the cost of the gilding of this temple in our days, it amounting to above twelve thousand **talents**.

[Omission for length]

Narration and Discussion

Plutarch says that Horatius was a man of "wonderful self-possession" (Dryden), or "a marvellous resolute man" (North). Do you think he believed what Marcus shouted out? Why might Marcus have done this?

Creative Narration: The temple scene might lend itself to dramatization, including (perhaps) official speeches telling some of its story so far. To go a bit further, you might include a bit of time-travelling (past to future, or future to past).

Word Study

Egg on: this has nothing to do with eggs! The word comes from "edge" or "urge."

Lesson Nine

Introduction

This lesson tells about two legendary Roman heroes.

In Part One, Tarquin attempted a comeback, with the aid of Lars

Porsena, an Etruscan ruler. When these demands were ignored, the Etruscans (sometimes called the Tuscans) made war on the Romans. Publicola defiantly built a fortified "city," Sigliuria, and filled it with Romans. However, like the story of the Three Little Pigs, the wolf arrived and they fled back to Rome. Both consuls were wounded while the war raged by the river; but a team of soldiers led by Horatius Cocles saved the bridge and the battle.

In Part Two, the Etruscans continued to besiege Rome; and a spy named Mucius found his way not only into the enemy camp, but right into Lars Porsena's war tent. As the Etruscans weren't wearing name tags, Mucius wasn't quite sure what to do next; but he did know how to improvise.

Vocabulary

retire: retreat

sallying out: rushing out

pike: spear

never changed hue nor countenance: never changed his expression; we might say "never batted an eye"

vanquished: overcome, conquered

treated with him of peace: negotiated peace terms with him

People

Lars Porsena [or Porsenna]: ruler of Clusium

Titus Lucretius: Titus Lucretius Triciptinus was consul with Publicola in 508 and 504 B.C.; this is not the same Lucretius who had died after replacing Collatinus

Athenodorus Cananites (74 B.C.-7 A.D.): a Stoic philosopher

Horatius Cocles: legendary for defending the *Pons Sublicius* (the earliest known bridge of Rome) from the Etruscan army

Cyclops: in Greek mythology, Cyclops had a single eye. The association of Cyclops with Horatius may be a later addition to the story.

Mucius: Gaius Mucius Cordus, later called Mucius Scaevola

Historic Occasions

ca. 508 B.C.: Etruscan attack on Rome

On the Map

Clusium: an Etruscan city

Sigliuria: fortified city built to demonstrate Roman power, which was then attacked by Porsena. There seems to be no definite answer to where it might have been, though a site called Satricum, south of Rome, is a possibility.

Reading

Part One: Horatius

Tarquin, after that great battle wherein he lost his son in combat with Brutus [**Lesson Five**], fled to the city of **Clusium**, and sought aid from **Lars Porsena**, then one of the most powerful princes of Italy, and a man of worth and generosity; who assured him of assistance, immediately sending his commands to Rome that they should receive Tarquin as their kin. Upon the Romans' refusal, [Porsena] proclaimed war; and, having signified the time and place where he intended his attack, approached with a great army.

Publicola was [though absent because of military duties] chosen consul a second time, and Titus Lucretius [was chosen as] his colleague. Returning to Rome, to show a spirit yet loftier than Porsena's, built the city **Sigliuria** when Porsena was already in the neighbourhood; and having walled it about to his marvellous charge, he sent seven hundred citizens to dwell there, to show that he made little account of this war. Nevertheless, Porsena, making a sharp assault, obliged the defendants to **retire** to Rome, who had almost in their entrance admitted the enemy into the city with them; only

Publicola, by **sallying out** at the gate, prevented them, and, joining battle by Tiber-side, opposed the enemy, that pressed on with their multitude; but at last, sinking under desperate wounds, [he] was carried out of the fight. And even so was the other consul **Lucretius** hurt in like case; so that the Romans, being dismayed, retreated into the city for their security, and Rome was in great hazard of being taken.

The enemy [forced] their way on to the wooden bridge, where **Horatius Cocles**, seconded by two of the first men in Rome, Herminius and Lartius, made head against them. (Horatius obtained this name from the loss of one of his eyes in the wars; or, as others write, from his flat nose which was so sunk into his head, that they saw nothing to part his eyes, but that the eyebrows did meet together; by reason whereof the people thinking to surname him **Cyclops**, by a mispronunciation they called him "Cocles.") This Cocles kept the bridge, and held back the enemy, till his own party broke it down behind. When he saw they had done that, armed as he was, and hurt in the hip with a **pike** of the Tuscans, he leaped into the Tiber, and saved himself by swimming unto the other side.

Publicola, admiring his courage, proposed at once that [every Roman] should make him a present of a day's provisions, and afterwards give him as much land as he could plough round in one day. Furthermore, he made his image of brass to be set up in the temple of Vulcan, comforting by this honour his wounded hip, whereof he was lame ever after.

Part Two: Mucius

But Porsena laying close siege to the city, and a famine raging amongst the Romans, [and] also a new army of the Tuscans making incursions into the country; Publicola, a third time chosen consul, designed to make, without sallying out, his defense against Porsena; but, privately stealing forth against the new army of the Tuscans, put them to flight and slew five thousand men.

As for the history of **Mucius**, many do diversely report it; but I will write it in such sort as I think shall best agree with the truth. This Mucius was a worthy man in all respects, but specially for the wars. He, resolving to kill Porsena, disguised himself in Tuscan apparel; and speaking Tuscan very perfectly, went into his camp, and came to the king's chair, in the which he gave audience; and not knowing him perfectly, he [dared] not ask which was he, least he should be discovered, but drew his sword and stabbed one who he thought had most the appearance of king.

Upon that they laid hold on him, and examined him. And a pan full of fire being brought for the king, that intended to do sacrifice unto the gods, Mucius held out his right hand over the fire, and, boldly looking the king full in his face, whilst the flesh of his hand did fry off, he **never changed hue nor countenance**. The king, wondering to see so strange a sight, called to them to withdraw the fire, and he himself did deliver him his sword again.

Mucius received it in his left hand, which occasioned the name of Scaevola, or "left-handed"; and said,

> I have overcome the terrors of Porsena, yet am **vanquished** by his generosity, and gratitude obliges me to disclose what no punishment could extort. Therefore for goodwill I will reveal that unto thee, which no force, nor extremity could have made me utter. There are three hundred Romans dispersed through thy camp, all which are prepared with like minds to follow that [which] I have begun, only gaping for opportunity to put it in practise. The lot fell on me to be the first to break the ice of this enterprise; and yet I am not sorry my hand failed to kill so worthy a man, that deserveth rather to be a friend than an enemy unto the Romans.

Porsena hearing this, did believe it, and ever after he gave the more willing ear to those that **treated with him of peace**: not so much (in my opinion) for that he feared the three hundred lying in wait to kill him, as for the admiration of the Roman's noble mind and great courage.

[short omission]

Narration and Discussion

Retell either of the stories from this passage, using one of the suggested creative extensions if you like.

Something to think about: If Mucius had handled himself with less courage, how might the story have ended differently?

Creative Narration #1: Act out one of the stories from this reading.

Creative Narration #2: Draw or paint an illustration.

Creative Narration #3: Thomas Babington Macaulay's famous poem "Horatius at the Bridge" is found in his book *Lays of Ancient Rome*. It begins,

> Lars Porsena of Clusium,
>> By the Nine Gods he swore
> That the great house of Tarquin
>> Should suffer wrong no more.
> By the Nine Gods he swore it,
>> And named a trysting-day,
> And bade his messengers ride forth,
> East and west and south and north,
>> To summon his array.

The whole poem is quite long, but you might choose part of it to read together, or to learn as memory work. How does Plutarch's account compare with Macaulay's? Are there parts of the story that you think might be legend, and why?

Creative Narration #4 (for older students): Write some verses in Macaulay's style but telling the story of Mucius.

Lesson Ten

Introduction

Publicola "took Tarquin to court" with Lars Porsena as judge, and together they made a peace treaty, with the main condition that

Tarquin (and his friends) would leave Rome to the Romans. As a gesture of good faith, Publicola agreed to send Porsena ten young people, including his daughter, as hostages. But things didn't work out quite as planned.

Vocabulary

controversy: dispute, quarrel

mistrusting the equity of his cause: thinking that perhaps Tarquin didn't have a very good case for being reinstated as king

equity: justice, fairness

patrician: noble

ambush: surprise attack. See **Word Study**.

skirmishing: fighting

sumptuously adorned: equipped with the finest harness, saddle, etc.

corn and other stores: grain and other useful supplies

Reading

Part One

But Publicola, taking King Porsena not to be so dangerous an enemy to Rome, as he should be a profitable friend and ally to the same: let him understand that he was contented to make him judge of the **controversy** between them and Tarquin. Several times [he] undertook to prove Tarquin the worst of men, and justly deprived of his kingdom. Tarquin sharply answered that he would make no man his judge, and Porsena least of all others: for, having promised him to put him again in his kingdom, he was now gone from his word, and had changed his mind.

Porsena, resenting this answer, and **mistrusting the equity of his cause**; [and] moved also by the solicitations of his son Aruns, who was earnest for the Roman interest; made a peace on these conditions: that they should resign the land they had taken from the Tuscans, restore all prisoners, and receive back their deserters. To confirm the peace, the Romans gave as hostages ten sons of **patrician** parents, and as many daughters, amongst whom was Valeria, the daughter of Publicola. Upon these assurances, Porsena [withdrew] his army, trusting to the peace concluded.

Part Two

The Romans' daughters, delivered for hostages, came down to the riverside to bathe, in a quiet place where the stream ran but gently, without any force or swiftness at all. When they were there, and saw they had no guard about them, nor any came that way, nor yet any boats going up nor down the stream: they had a desire to swim over the river, which ran with a swift stream, and was marvellous deep. Some say, that one of them, by name Cloelia, passing over on horseback, persuaded the rest to swim after; but, upon their safe arrival, presenting themselves to Publicola, he neither praised nor approved their return but was concerned lest he should appear less faithful than Porsena; and this boldness in the maidens should argue treachery in the Romans; so that, apprehending them, he sent them back to Porsena.

But Tarquin's men, having intelligence of this, laid an **ambush** on the other side for those that conducted them; and while these were **skirmishing** together, Valeria, the daughter of Publicola, rushed through the enemy, and fled, and with the assistance of three of her attendants made good her escape, whilst the rest were dangerously hedged in by the soldiers. Aruns, Porsena's son, upon tidings of it, hastened to their rescue; but when he came, the enemies fled, and the Romans held on their journey to redeliver their hostages.

When Porsena saw the maidens returned, demanding who was the author and adviser of the act, and understanding Cloelia to be the person, he looked on her very earnestly and with a pleasant countenance; and, commanding one of his horses to be brought, **sumptuously adorned**, made her a present of it. This is produced as evidence by those who affirm that only Cloelia passed the river on horseback; those who deny it call it only the honour the Tuscan did to her courage. A figure, however, on horseback, stands in the Via Sacra, as you go to the Palatium, which some say is the statue of Cloelia, others of Valeria.

Porsena, thus reconciled to the Romans, gave them a fresh instance of his generosity, and commanded his soldiers to quit the camp merely with their armour and weapons, leaving their tents, full of **corn and other stores**, as a gift to the Romans. Hence even down to our time, when there is a public sale of goods, they cry that they are King Porsena's goods, by way of perpetual commemoration of his kindness. There stood also, by the senate-house, a brazen statue of him, of plain and antique workmanship.

Narration and Discussion

Why did Porsena require the Romans to send him the young people as hostages? What does it say about Publicola's character that he would send his own daughter, and that he would send her back again after she escaped?

Who do you think was the bravest person in this story?

Creative Narration: Imagine (write, act out, illustrate) the scene between father and daughter when Valeria showed up at home after her swim across the river.

For further thought: Restate this in your own words: "But Publicola taking King Porsena not to be so dangerous an enemy to Rome, as he should be a profitable friend and ally to the same..." Do you agree with Publicola's judgement here, or Plutarch's interpretation of it? (In fact, Porsena could have been extremely dangerous; some sources say that he may even have ruled in Rome himself for a short time.)

Word Study

Ambush: hiding and lying in wait to make an attack. This comes from a Middle French word, *embuschier*, which literally means "to set in the woods." In Latin, *busca* means woods or forest.

Lesson Eleven

Introduction

There are two distinct periods covered here: first, the year that Publicola was not consul at all (his brother Marcus was elected instead), and two years after that, when Publicola was consul for the fourth time.

The Sabines continued to attack Rome, but under Marcus (with Publicola's help), Rome won a great victory. The next year, under Publicola, Rome was threatened by an attack by the Sabines and the Latins combined; and the people were also discouraged by signs that the gods seemed to be against them. Publicola handled both situations with his usual calm leadership

Vocabulary

dissuading: speaking against, discouraging

gave easy ear unto such speeches: were ready to pay attention

sedition: uprising, rebellion

despatched emissaries: sent messengers

making virtue of necessity: making the best of a bad situation

admitted them...to the franchise: made them honourary citizens

Historic Occasions

506 B.C.: Marcus Valerius defended Rome against the Sabines

504 B.C.: Publicola elected consul for the fourth time

504 B.C.: Publicola's triumph for victory over the Sabines

On the Map

River Anio: now called the Aniene (formerly the Teverone); a river which flows westward to join the Tiber in northern Rome

Reading

Part One

Afterwards, the **Sabines** invading the Romans' territory with a great force, Marcus Valerius, Publicola's brother, was then chosen consul, with one Postumius Tubertus. Marcus, through the management of affairs by the conduct and direct assistance of Publicola, obtained two great victories, in the latter of which he slew thirteen thousand Sabines without the loss of one Roman, and was honoured, as an accession to his triumph, with a house built in the Palatium at the public charge; and whereas the doors of other houses opened inward into the house, they made this to open outward into the street, to intimate their perpetual public recognition of his merit by thus continually making way for him. (The same fashion in their doors the Greeks, they say, had of old universally, which appears from their comedies, where those that are going out make a noise at the door within, to give notice to those that pass by or stand near the door, that the opening the door into the street might occasion no surprise.)

Part Two

The next year after that, Publicola was chosen consul the fourth time, when a confederacy of the Sabines and Latins threatened a war *[omission for content]*. Now there was at that time amongst the Sabines, a great rich man called Appius Clausus, a man of a great wealth and strength of body, but most eminent for his high character and for his eloquence; yet, as is usually the fate of great men, he could not escape the envy of others, which was much occasioned by his **dissuading** the war. Whereupon, many which before took occasion to murmur against him, did now much more increase the same: with saying he sought to maintain the power of the Romans, that afterwards by [Roman] aid he might make himself tyrant and king of the country. The common people **gave easy ear unto such speeches**, and Appius, perceiving well enough how the soldiers hated him, feared they would complain and accuse him. But, having a considerable body of friends and allies to assist him, he raised a tumult amongst the Sabines, which delayed the war.

Publicola, also for his part, was very diligent not only to understand the original cause of the **sedition**, but to promote and increase it; and he **despatched emissaries** with instructions to Clausus, that Publicola was assured of his goodness and justice, and thought it indeed unworthy in any man, however injured, to seek revenge upon his fellow-citizens; yet if he pleased, for his own security, to leave his enemies and come to Rome, he should be received, both in public and private, with the honour his merit deserved, and their own glory required.

Appius Clausus having long and many times considered this matter with himself, resolved that it was the best way he could take, **making virtue of necessity**; and advising with his friends, and they inviting again others in the same manner, he came to Rome, bringing five thousand families, with their wives and children, people of the quietest and steadiest temper of all the Sabines.

Publicola, informed of their approach, received them with all the kind offices of a friend; and **admitted them at once to the franchise**, allotting to every one two acres of land by the **River Anio**. But to Clausus [he gave] twenty-five acres, and a place in the Senate: a commencement of political power which he used so wisely, that he rose to the highest reputation, was very influential, and left the Claudian house behind him, inferior to none in Rome.

Narration and Discussion

Why was Publicola not only happy to hear about the turmoil between the various groups of Sabines, but eager to encourage it? What do you think his motives were for inviting the Clausus family (actually five thousand families!) to come to Rome? What were some of the problems they may have encountered?

Creative Narration: Tell the story of the (extremely large) Appius Clausus family, preparing to "emigrate" to Rome. What might the Romans have thought about this? One possible conversation might be between children or teenagers, the established gang and the "new kids on the block." Another might be a dinner-table conversation about the new family down the street.

For further thought (for older students): Why did the Sabines mistrust the intentions of Appius Clausus? How might he have defended his position on the war?

Lesson Twelve

Introduction

Part One of this lesson is about the Sabines and their revenge on the Romans.

Part Two is about the death and funeral of Publicola, "the object of universal regret and sorrow."

Vocabulary

ambuscade: ambush

advertised: warned, informed

encompassed: surrounded

betimes: early

straight break: break up and flee

albeit: although

spoil: loot, treasure

public interment: burial at the public expense

posterity: descendants

Historic Occasions

503 B.C.: Death of Publicola

On the Map

Fidenae: a town about 5 miles (8 km) north of Rome

Reading

Part One

The departure of these men rendered things quiet amongst the Sabines; yet the chief of the community would not suffer them to settle into peace, but resented that Clausus now, by turning deserter, should disappoint that revenge upon the Romans which, while at home, he had unsuccessfully opposed. Coming with a great army, they sat down before **Fidenae**, and placed an **ambuscade** of two thousand men near Rome, in wooded and hollow spots, with a design that some few horsemen, as soon as it was day, should go out and ravage the country, commending them, that when the Romans came out of the city to charge them, they should seem leisurely to retire, until they had drawn them within danger of their ambush.

Publicola, however, soon **advertised** of these designs by deserters, divided his army in two parts. He gave his son-in-law, Postumius Balbus, three thousand footmen, whom he sent away by night, commanding them to take the hills, under which the ambush lay, there to observe their motions; his colleague, Lucretius, attended with a body of the lightest and boldest men, was appointed to meet the Sabine horse; whilst he, with the rest of the army, **encompassed** the enemy.

The next morning **betimes**, by chance it was a thick mist, and at that present time Postumius coming down from the hills, with great shouts, charged them that lay in ambush.

Lucretius, on the other side, set upon the light horsemen of the Sabines; and Publicola fell upon their camp. So that of all sides the Sabines' enterprise had very ill success, for they had the worst in every place, and the Romans killed them flying, without any turning again to make resistance.

Thus the place which gave them hope of best safety, turned most to their deadly overthrow. For every one of their companies supposing the other had been whole and unbroken, when a charge was given upon them, did **straight break**, and never a company of them turned

59

head toward their enemy. For they that were in the camp, ran toward them which lay in ambush: and those which were in ambush on the contrary side, ran towards them that were in camp. So that in flying, the one met with the other, and found those towards whom they were flying to have been safe, to stand in as much need of help as themselves.

The nearness, however, of the city Fidenae was the preservation of the Sabines, especially those that fled from the camp: those that could not gain the city either perished in the field, or were taken prisoners. As for the glory of this honourable victory, **albeit** the Romans were wont to ascribe all such great notable matters to the special providence and grace of the gods; yet at that time notwithstanding they did judge, that this happy success fell out by the wise foresight and valiantness of the captain. For every man that had served in this journey had no other talk in his mouth, but that Publicola had delivered their enemies into their hands *[short omission]*. The people were marvellously enriched by this victory, as well for the **spoil** as for the ransom of the prisoners that they had gotten.

Part Two

Publicola, having completed his triumph, and bequeathed the city to the care of the succeeding consuls, died; thus closing a life which, as far as human life may be, had been full of all that is good and honourable.

The people, as though they had not duly rewarded his deserts when alive, but still were in his debt, decreed him a **public interment**, every one contributing towards the charge; the women, besides, by private consent, mourned a whole year, a signal mark of honour to his memory.

He was buried, by the people's desire, within the city, in the part called Velia, where his **posterity** had likewise privilege of burial.

[omission for length]

Narration and Discussion

As Plutarch said, success in battle was often attributed to the favour of the gods. Why was Publicola's last battle "attributed to the conduct of one captain?"

How was Publicola honoured after his death?

Creative Narration: This lesson may be extended artistically, dramatically, or in any format that seems a good way to wind up the study.

For further thought: In Plutarch's comparison of Solon and Publicola, he quotes Solon as saying "Both great and small of power, the better will obey: / if we too little or too much, upon them do not lay." Dryden translates this, "A people always minds its rulers best / When it is neither humoured nor oppressed." How is that a fitting description of Publicola?

Plutarch ends his comparison of Solon and Publicola with this:

> "For the King their enemy did not only make peace
> with them, but did also leave them all his furniture,
> provision, and munition for the wars; even for the
> virtue, manhood, and justice, which the great
> wisdom of this consul persuaded Porsena to believe
> to be, in all the other Romans."

Dryden translates this as "the virtue and gallant disposition of the Romans," of which Publicola could be taken as a prime example. How do those words fit the picture Plutarch has given us of Publicola?

For further thought (for older students): Imagine that Publicola had come across a copy of the book of Proverbs. What might have been some of his favorite verses? Do you think there are any proverbs that might have bothered him or made him wonder if his life really was "full of all that is good and honourable?"

Examination Questions

You may choose from any of these questions, or write your own.

Younger Students:

1. Why did Valerius/Publicola expect he would become one of the first consuls of the Roman Republic? What actually happened?

2. Tell about one of these people: a) Publicola's daughter Valeria, b) Mucius Scaevola, or c) Vindicius.

3. How did Publicola make life better for the Roman people?

Older Students:

1. The Romans believed that "the gods" seemed to favour Publicola. To what do you attribute his success as a leader: supernatural help (from God or the gods), or his own character and ability? Give examples.

2. How did life in Rome change during Publicola's lifetime?

3. Tell the story of a) the young maidens sent as hostages or b) Mucius in the camp of Lars Porsena.

Made in the USA
Monee, IL
15 July 2024